Kenny

by Iain Gray

LangSyne
PUBLISHING
WRITING *to* REMEMBER

LangSyne

PUBLISHING

WRITING *to* REMEMBER

Vineyard Business Centre,
Pathhead, Midlothian EH37 5XP
Tel: 01875 321 203 Fax: 01875 321 233
E-mail: info@lang-syne.co.uk
www.langsyneshop.co.uk

Design by Dorothy Meikle
Printed by Ricoh Print Scotland
© Lang Syne Publishers Ltd 2011

ISBN 978-1-85217-406-4

Kenny

MOTTO:
May it hold and shine
(or) May it hold, shine and flourish,
by valour virtue and worth.

CREST:
An arm in armour, grasping a scroll.

NAME variations include:

Keany	MacKenny
Keaney	O'Kenny
Keeney	O'Kinney
Kenney	Ó Cionaith *(Gaelic)*
Kennie	Ó Cionnaith, *(Gaelic)*
Kinney	Ó Cionaodha *(Gaelic)*
Kinnie	Ó Cionnaoith *(Gaelic)*
MacKeany	Ó Coinnigh *(Gaelic)*
McKenny	

Chapter one:
Origins of Irish surnames

According to an old saying, there are two types of Irish – those who actually are Irish and those who wish they were.

This sentiment is only one example of the allure that the high romance and drama of the proud nation's history holds for thousands of people scattered across the world today.

It's a sad fact, however, that the vast majority of Irish surnames are found far beyond Irish shores, rather than on the Emerald Isle itself.

The population stood at around eight million souls in 1841, but today it stands at fewer than six million.

This is mainly a tragic consequence of the potato famine, also known as the Great Hunger, which devastated Ireland between 1845 and 1849.

The Irish peasantry had become almost wholly reliant for basic sustenance on the potato, first introduced from the Americas in the seventeenth century.

When the crop was hit by a blight, at least 800,000 people starved to death while an estimated two million others were forced to seek a new life far from their native shores – particularly in America, Canada, and Australia.

The effects of the potato blight continued until about 1851, by which time a firm pattern of emigration had become established.

Ireland's loss, however, was to the gain of the countries in which the immigrants settled, contributing enormously, as their descendants do today, to the well being of the nations in which their forefathers settled.

But those who were forced through dire circumstance to establish a new life in foreign parts never forgot their roots, or the proud heritage and traditions of the land that gave them birth.

Nor do their descendants.

It is a heritage that is inextricably bound up in the colourful variety of Irish names themselves – and the origin and history of these names forms an integral part of the vibrant drama that is the nation's history, one of both glorious fortune and tragic misfortune.

This history is well documented, and one of the most important and fascinating of the earliest sources are *The Annals of the Four Masters*, compiled between 1632 and 1636 by four friars at the Franciscan Monastery in County Donegal.

Compiled from earlier sources, and purporting to go back to the Biblical Deluge, much of the material takes in the mythological origins and history of Ireland and the Irish.

This includes tales of successive waves of invaders and settlers such as the Fomorians, the Partholonians, the Nemedians, the Fir Bolgs, the Tuatha De Danann, and the Laigain.

Of particular interest are the *Milesian Genealogies*,

because the majority of Irish clans today claim a descent from either Heremon, Ir, or Heber – three of the sons of Milesius, a king of what is now modern day Spain.

These sons invaded Ireland in the second millennium B.C, apparently in fulfilment of a mysterious prophecy received by their father.

This Milesian lineage is said to have ruled Ireland for nearly 3,000 years, until the island came under the sway of England's King Henry II in 1171 following what is known as the Cambro-Norman invasion.

This is an important date not only in Irish history in general, but for the effect the invasion subsequently had for Irish surnames.

'Cambro' comes from the Welsh, and 'Cambro-Norman' describes those Welsh knights of Norman origin who invaded Ireland.

But they were invaders who stayed, inter-marrying with the native Irish population and founding their own proud dynasties that bore Cambro-Norman names such as Archer, Barbour, Brannagh, Fitzgerald, Fitzgibbon, Fleming, Joyce, Plunkett, and Walsh – to name only a few.

These 'Cambro-Norman' surnames that still flourish throughout the world today form one of the three main categories in which Irish names can be placed – those of Gaelic-Irish, Cambro-Norman, and Anglo-Irish.

Previous to the Cambro-Norman invasion of the twelfth century, and throughout the earlier invasions and settlement of those wild bands of sea rovers known as the Vikings in the eighth and ninth centuries, the population of the island was relatively small, and it was normal for a person to be identified through the use of only a forename.

But as population gradually increased and there were many more people with the same forename, surnames were adopted to distinguish one person, or one community, from another.

Individuals identified themselves with their own particular tribe, or 'tuath', and this tribe – that also became known as a clann, or clan – took its name from some distinguished ancestor who had founded the clan.

The Gaelic-Irish form of the name Kelly, for example, is Ó Ceallaigh, or O'Kelly, indicating descent from an original 'Ceallaigh', with the 'O' denoting 'grandson of.' The name was later anglicised to Kelly.

The prefix 'Mac' or 'Mc', meanwhile, as with the clans of the Scottish Highlands, denotes 'son of.'

Although the Irish clans had much in common with their Scottish counterparts, one important difference lies in what are known as 'septs', or branches, of the clan.

Septs of Scottish clans were groups who often bore an entirely different name from the clan name but were under the clan's protection.

In Ireland, septs were groups that shared the same name and who could be found scattered throughout the four provinces of Ulster, Leinster, Munster, and Connacht.

The 'golden age' of the Gaelic-Irish clans, infused as their veins were with the blood of Celts, pre-dates the Viking invasions of the eighth and ninth centuries and the Norman invasion of the twelfth century, and the sacred heart of the country was the Hill of Tara, near the River Boyne, in County Meath.

Known in Gaelic as 'Teamhar na Rí', or Hill of Kings, it was the royal seat of the 'Ard Rí Éireann', or High King of Ireland, to whom the petty kings, or chieftains, from the island's provinces were ultimately subordinate.

It was on the Hill of Tara, beside a stone pillar known as the Irish 'Lia Fáil', or Stone of Destiny, that the High Kings were inaugurated and, according to legend, this stone would emit a piercing screech that could be heard all over Ireland when touched by the hand of the rightful king.

The Hill of Tara is today one of the island's main tourist attractions.

Opposition to English rule over Ireland, established in the wake of the Cambro-Norman invasion, broke out frequently and the harsh solution adopted by the powerful forces of the Crown was to forcibly evict the native Irish from their lands.

These lands were then granted to Protestant colonists, or 'planters', from Britain.

Many of these colonists, ironically, came from Scotland and were the descendants of the original 'Scotti', or 'Scots', who gave their name to Scotland after migrating there in the fifth century A.D., from the north of Ireland.

Colonisation entailed harsh penal laws being imposed on the majority of the native Irish population, stripping them practically of all of their rights.

The Crown's main bastion in Ireland was Dublin and its environs, known as the Pale, and it was the dispossessed peasantry who lived outside this Pale, desperately striving to eke out a meagre living.

It was this that gave rise to the modern-day expression of someone or something being 'beyond the pale'.

Attempts were made to stamp out all aspects of the ancient Gaelic-Irish culture, to the extent that even to bear a Gaelic-Irish name was to invite discrimination.

This is why many Gaelic-Irish names were anglicised with, for example, and noted above, Ó Ceallaigh, or O'Kelly, being anglicised to Kelly.

Succeeding centuries have seen strong revivals of Gaelic-Irish consciousness, however, and this has led to many families reverting back to the original form of their name, while the language itself is frequently found on the fluent tongues of an estimated 90,000 to 145,000 of the island's population.

Ireland's turbulent history of religious and political strife is one that lasted well into the twentieth century, a landmark century that saw the partition of the island into the twenty-six counties of the independent Republic of

Ireland, or Eire, and the six counties of Northern Ireland, or Ulster.

Dublin, originally founded by Vikings, is now a vibrant and truly cosmopolitan city while the proud city of Belfast is one of the jewels in the crown of Ulster.

It was Saint Patrick who first brought the light of Christianity to Ireland in the fifth century A.D.

Interpretations of this Christian message have varied over the centuries, often leading to bitter sectarian conflict – but the many intricately sculpted Celtic Crosses found all over the island are symbolic of a unity that crosses the sectarian divide.

It is an image that fuses the 'old gods' of the Celts with Christianity.

All the signs from the early years of this new millennium indicate that sectarian strife may soon become a thing of the past – with the Irish and their many kinsfolk across the world, be they Protestant or Catholic, finding common purpose in the rich tapestry of their shared heritage.

Chapter two:

Born of fire

**A name with an ancient and illustrious pedigree, Kenny
and its equally popular spelling variations is the
anglicised version of a number of Gaelic-Irish forms
that include Ó Cionaith and Ó Cionnaoith.**

Thought to have derived from pre-Christian, or pagan,
roots from Ó Cionaodha, with 'aodh' indicating the ancient
Celtic sun god Aodh, this may explain why the name is
thought to mean 'fire-sprung', 'fiery sun', or 'born of fire'.

A Gaelic-Scottish version of the name, 'Coinneach',
meanwhile indicates 'son of the fair one.'

'Kenny' is a diminutive, or shortened, version of the
popular forename Kenneth and its 'nickname' derivatives of
'Ken' and 'Kenny' – while there was also a real historical
bearer of the name of 'Kenneth' who popularised the name
both as a first name and, later, as a surname.

Ironically, perhaps, in view of the pagan origins of the
name, this identifiable historical figure was the sixth century
Irish Christian missionary known in his native Gaelic
tongue as Cainnech of Aghaboe – better known as
St Canice, or St Kenneth, and who gave his name to the city
and counties of Kilkenny, in the Irish Republic.

'Kilkenny' is derived from 'Cill Chainnigh', anglicised
as 'Church of Kenneth', and it was here, in the late sixth

century, that he founded the monastery on whose original site St Canice's Cathedral proudly flourishes against the skyline today.

Again, perhaps ironically considering the pagan roots of his name, St Canice established the Christian church that gave its name to Kilkenny after leading a victorious force to defeat what was then one of the last few remaining seats of the ancient Druidic cult.

In common with many other Druidic sites that represented the mystical 'old religion' of the Celts, this site was subsequently 'hijacked' to incorporate and represent the 'new god' of Christianity.

One example of how Christianity successfully repressed the cult of the Druids can be identified through the enduring myth that it was the fifth century Christian missionary St Patrick who 'banished' serpents from the Emerald Isle.

Serpents were identified from ancient times in a number of belief systems including those of the Egyptians and the Druids, as symbolic of knowledge and wisdom.

The historical truth is that what is really meant by saying that St Patrick 'freed Ireland from serpents' is that he, and succeeding Christian missionaries such as St Canice, eradicated the serpent-worshipping Druids from the Emerald Isle.

Thought to have been born about 515 A.D. near Dungiven, St Canice, or Kenneth, whose feast day is October 11, not only undertook missionary work in Ireland but also in Scotland – where his name survives on the landscape today in a number of forms that include Inch Kenneth, off the west coast island of Mull and the ancient burial ground on the sacred island of Iona known as Kil-Chainnech.

Recognised, along with other saints that include his contemporary St Columcille, or Columba, as one of the Twelve Apostles of Ireland, before his death in 600 A.D. he also founded the monastery and abbey of Aghaboe, in modern day Co. Laois, and wrote an influential commentary on the gospels known as *Glas-Choinnigh*, or the *Chain of Cainnech*.

In common with other native Irish clans that include those of O'Branagan, Quinn and Moran, the Kennys also trace a proud descent from a son of Milesius.

This king of what is now modern day Spain had planned to invade Ireland in fulfilment of a mysterious Druidic prophecy.

He died before he could launch the invasion but his sons, including Heber, Ir, Heremon and Amergin, successfully undertook the daunting task in his stead in about 1699B.C.

Legend holds that their invasion fleet was scattered in a storm and Ir killed when his ship was driven onto the island of Scellig-Mhicheal, off the coast of modern day Co. Kerry.

Of the brothers, only Heremon, Heber and Amergin survived, although Ir left sons.

Heremon and Heber became the first of the Milesian monarchs of Ireland, but Heremon later killed Heber in a quarrel said to have been caused by their wives, while Amergin was slain by Heremon in an argument over territory.

It is from the offspring of Ir that the Kennys of today trace their ancient and royal lineage.

The main territories of the Kennys were the present day counties of Galway and Roscommon, in the province of Connacht, while they were also to be found in other areas that include modern day Co. Donegal, where they were recognised as Lords of Muinter Kenny, and in the Ulster counties of Down and Tyrone.

The most prominent grouping of the Kennys, or Ó Coinnaoiths, was that which flourished as part of the mighty tribal grouping known as the Uí Maine that traced a descent back to the mid-fourth century warrior king Maine Mór.

'Uí Maine' (also known as Hy Many) means 'Maine's territory', and this was a vast kingdom that comprised the bulk of Connacht.

Clans such as the Kennys who formed part of the Uí Maine enjoyed special privileges – such as being given a choice to go into battle on behalf of their king in either spring or autumn, and therefore allowing them a period to cultivate and tend their crops.

The Uí Maine monarchs also enjoyed rights that included 'a portion of all prizes and wrecks of the sea', all the province's gold and silver mines and 'hidden treasures found underground.'

As part of the Uí Maine, the Kennys were at the forefront of the bloody struggles to maintain their ancient rights and privileges and Gaelic way of life that followed the late twelfth century Cambro-Norman invasion of the island and the subsequent consolidation of the power of the English Crown.

By historical coincidence, one of the English families to benefit from the Crown's domination of Ireland was named Kenny.

Originally from Somerset, and descended from Nicholas Kenny, who held a powerful Crown post on the island during the late sixteenth century, their descendants are to be found to this day mainly in the original native Irish Kenny homelands of Galway and Roscommon.

Whatever their roots, bearers of the Kenny name and its variations have left a significant impression both in Ireland and further afield through a number of endeavours.

In political activism, Henry Kenny, born in 1913, was the Irish politician who served as the Fine Gael TD (member) for Mayo in the Republic of Ireland Parliament, Dáil Éireann, from 1954 until his death in 1975.

Also a Gaelic footballer who was a winner of an All-Ireland medal in 1936 with the Mayo inter-county team, he was the father of Irish politician Enda Kenny, born in 1951 in Castlebar, Co. Mayo.

Succeeding his father as TD for Mayo in a by-election following his death, Enda Kenny served from 1994 to 1997 as the Irish Republic's Minister for Tourism and Trade, while he was appointed leader of Fine Gael in 2002.

Known by one of the Irish-Gaelic versions of the Kenny name, Seán Ó Cionnaith was the prominent Irish socialist republican politician who was born in 1938 near Ballinasloe, Co. Galway.

Closely involved throughout his political career with organisations that included Sinn Fein and the Northern Ireland Civil Rights Association, he died in 2003.

One particularly feisty bearer of the Kenny name – in this case in the form of the popular spelling variation of Kenney – Annie Kenney was the influential English campaigner for voting rights for women who was born in 1879 in Saddleworth, Yorkshire.

As a member of the suffragette movement, she is recognised as having initiated the movement's militant activity when, in October of 1915 and to the outrage of the establishment of the time, she and Christabel Pankhurst heckled Winston Churchill and fellow politician Sir Edward Grey during a Liberal Party rally in Manchester.

This was an act that resulted in the former cotton mill worker being sentenced to three days imprisonment – the first of a number of prison sentences she served for her political activism on behalf of women's rights.

She died in 1953.

Chapter three:

Honours and accolades

On the field of battle, no less than six bearers of the Kenny name have gained distinction through being recipients of the Victoria Cross (VC), the highest award for bravery in the face of enemy action for British and Commonwealth troops.

Born in 1831 in Dublin, James Kenny was a private in the 53rd Regiment of Foot during the Indian Mutiny of 1857-1858 when, in November of 1857 during an assault on the Secundra Bagh during the Relief of Lucknow, he received the VC after bringing up ammunition for his company under very heavy cross-fire.

He was killed five years later in another military action in India.

Also in India, William David Kenny, born in 1899 in Saintfield, Co. Down, was a posthumous Irish recipient of the VC.

A lieutenant in the 4/39th Garhwal Rifles, Indian Army, during the Waziristan Campaign, he was killed in January 1920 after leading a diversionary attack on the enemy, allowing wounded comrades to be withdrawn to safety; his VC is on display at the National Army Museum in Chelsea.

During the First World War, bearers of the Kenny name won four other Victoria Crosses.

Born in 1888 in Hackney, London, Henry Kenny was a private in the 1st Battalion, Loyal North Lancashire Regiment when, in September of 1915 near Loos, in France, he braved enemy fire on six separate occasions to single-handedly bring back wounded comrades to the safety of the British lines.

Later reaching the rank of sergeant, he died in 1979.

Thomas Kenny, also known as Bede Kenny, was an Australian recipient of the VC.

He had been a private in the 2nd Battalion (New South Wales) Australian Imperial Force when, in April of 1917 at Hermiès, France, he stormed and bombed an enemy gun emplacement; he died in 1953.

Another Thomas Kenny was also a recipient of the VC.

Born in 1882 in Co. Durham, he had been a private in the 13th Battalion, The Durham Light Infantry when, in November of 1915 near La Houssoie, France, at great risk to himself, he rescued a wounded officer from the battlefield; he died in 1948.

Yet another Irish recipient of the VC was William Kenny, who was born in 1880 in Drogheda, Co. Louth.

A drummer in the 2nd Battalion, The Gordon Highlanders, it was near Ypres, in Belgium, in October of 1914 that he not only rescued wounded comrades on five separate occasions but also managed to convey urgent messages between his battalion's positions.

Later promoted to Drum Major, he died in 1936.

Born in 1889 in Yarmouth, Nova Scotia, and later settling in the United States, George C. Kenny was a highly decorated United States Army Air Forces (USAAF) general.

Serving with the Aviation Section, U.S. Signal Corps during the First World War, he flew a number of combat missions and is credited with having shot down Hermann Goering, later head of Nazi Germany's Luftwaffe.

Serving from 1942 to 1945 as Commander of Allied Forces in the South West Pacific, the general, who later wrote three books about his experiences, died in 1977.

Continuing the Kenny military tradition, Sir Brian Kenny, born in 1934, is the retired British Army general who served as Deputy Supreme Allied Commander Europe from 1990 to 1993 and as Governor of the Royal Hospital, Chelsea, from 1993 to 1999.

From the destructive art of war to the more constructive art of healing, one of the most remarkable bearers of the name and one whose legacy endures to this day to the benefit of millions of people worldwide was Elizabeth Kenny.

Born in 1880 of Irish stock in Warialda, New South Wales, and later settling with her family in the village of Nobby, in Queensland, she is recognised as having pioneered the technique of muscle rehabilitation known as physical therapy, or physiotherapy, despite having had no formal medical education.

It was while being treated as a 14-year-old for a broken

wrist that she became fascinated with the model skeleton in her doctor's clinic; unable to buy one, she made her own, while studying books on anatomy to determine how muscles function.

By the age of 21 she was working as an unofficial bush nurse in Nobby, eventually opening a small cottage hospital in the nearby village of Clifton, where she used her muscle rehabilitation techniques to treat people suffering from polio.

Although lacking medical qualifications, she was accepted as a nurse during the First World War on what were known as the Dark Ships – troop transports that sailed between Australia and Britain with all lights extinguished to evade enemy attacks.

These vessels carried trade goods and soldiers to Britain and, on the return voyage, wounded combatants and, in 1917, the Australian Army Nurse Corps granted her the title of Sister.

Returning to Nobby at the end of the conflict, Sister Kenny later invented her own form of stretcher for use with ambulances.

Named the Sylvia Stretcher, after one of her young patients, it sold in substantial numbers throughout Australia, Europe and the United States, with the profits donated to the Australian Country Women's Association.

Developing and perfecting her clinical technique of muscle rehabilitation, or physiotherapy, she wrote a best-selling book on the subject in 1937 and later travelled extensively throughout her native Australia and much further afield, explaining her technique and setting up clinics.

Although her technique often proved controversial with the medical establishment – for example, she was opposed to restraining children's muscle action with braces or plaster casts – it spread rapidly in popularity and is recognised as being responsible for the successful treatment of millions of polio sufferers across the world.

One of the many people to have benefited from the technique is the American actor Alan Alda, who is on record as crediting it for his complete recovery from polio as a child.

The story of this mainly self-taught nurse from a small Australian community caught the popular imagination and found its way onto the silver screen in 1946, six years before her death, as the film *Sister Kenny*, with Rosalind Russell in the title role.

Chapter four:
On the world stage

From music and sport to acting and literature, bearers of the Kenny name and its rich number of spelling variations have achieved international recognition.

A singer and songwriter who has penned hits for a number of artists, **Gerard Kenny** was born in 1947 in New York.

Settling in London in the early 1970s, one of his best-known songs is *I Could Be So Good For You*, the theme tune for the British television series *Minder*.

Performed by *Minder* actor Dennis Waterman, the song won Kenny an Ivor Novello Award for song writing, while American singer Barry Manilow performed his hit composition *I Made It Through The Rain*.

As a singer in his own right, he enjoyed hits with his 1978 *New York, New York* and the 1980 *Fantasy* while, along with singer-songwriter Lynsey de Paul, he co-wrote Shirley Bassey's *There's No Place Like London*.

In folk music, **Enda Kenny**, who was born in Dublin but immigrated to Melbourne, Australia, in 1987, is the singer and songwriter whose best-selling albums include his 1994 *Twelve Songs* and, from 2005, *Here and There*.

A newspaper columnist and poet in addition to noted song lyricist, **Nick Kenny** was born in 1895 in Astoria, New York.

Following a spell in the United States Navy followed by the Merchant Marine, during which time he began writing poems, he joined the staff of the *Bayonne Times* in 1920 and later worked for other newspapers that included the *New York Daily News* and the *Sarasota Herald Tribune*.

As a song lyricist, he is best known for *Gold Mine in the Sky*, which inspired the 1938 Gene Autry film of that name and, from 1957, the Pat Boone hit *Love Letters in the Sand*.

Host from 1951 to 1952 of his own American television music and talk show and author of collections of poetry that include *The Navy in Rhyme* and *Day Unto Day*, he died in 1975.

Born in 1910 in Toronto, **Mart Kenney** was the Canadian jazz saxophonist, clarinettist and bandleader who in 1931 founded the popular dance band Mart Kenney and His Western Gentlemen.

The band, in addition to live appearances and broadcasts for radio, also enjoyed a string of hits that include *There's Honey on the Moon Tonight*.

Made a Member of the Order of Canada in 1980, he died in 2006.

Bearers of the Kenny name, in all its variety of spellings, have also excelled, and continue to excel, in the highly competitive world of sport, not least in their original homeland of Ireland.

In the fast paced game of hurling, **Paddy Kenny**, born in 1929 in Borrisoleigh, Co. Tipperary, played for both his local Borrisoleigh club and the Tipperary senior inter-county team throughout the 1940s and 1950s.

Regarded as one of Tipperary's greatest players of all time, he died in 2004.

Also from Borrisoleigh and six years younger than Paddy Kenny, **Seán Kenny** was the captain of the Tipperary team that took the All-Ireland title in 1950; he died in 2002.

Not only talented in hurling but also in Gaelic football, **Tom Kenny**, born in 1981 in Grenagh, Co. Cork, has played since 2003 with the Cork senior inter-county teams for both sports.

On the fields of European football, **Stephen Kenny** is the former footballer turned manager who was born in 1971 in Dublin.

As a player, he played for teams that include Derry City and St Patrick's Athletic, while teams he has managed include Derry City and Scottish club Dunfermline Athletic.

A midfielder for teams that include English clubs Liverpool and Crewe, **Mark Kenny**, born in 1973 in Dublin, also played for the League of Ireland for Shamrock Rovers from 1996 to 2005 and, at the time of writing, is coach for Phoenix F.C. in the Leinster Senior League.

Born in 1978 in Halifax, West Yorkshire, **Paddy Kenny** is the goalkeeper who has played for English teams that include Sheffield United and Queens Park Rangers.

It is because both of his parents are Irish that he also qualified to play, between 2004 and 2006, for the Republic of Ireland national team, earning seven caps.

In the much different game of American football, **Bill Kenney**, born in 1955 in San Francisco, is the retired quarterback who played for teams that include the Miami Dolphins, Kansas City Chieftains and Washington Redskins.

Turning to politics after retiring from the game, he served as the Republican majority floor leader in the Missouri Senate from 2001 to 2003.

On the cycling track, **Jason Kenny** is the English track cyclist who was born in 1988 in Bolton and who, along with team mates Chris Hoy and Jamie Staff, won a gold medal in the team sprint event and silver in the individual sprint at the 2008 Olympic Games in Beijing.

In the Canadian national sport of ice hockey, **Jim McKenny**, nicknamed "Howie" and who was born in 1946 in Ottawa, is the retired National Hockey League defenceman who, from 1965 to 1979, played for teams that include the Toronto Maple Leafs, Minnesota North Stars and Vancouver Canucks.

From ice hockey to the rough and tumble of rugby league, **Brett Kenny**, born in 1969 in Gerringong, New South Wales, is ranked as one of Australia's finest players of the twentieth century.

He played throughout the 1980s and 1990s for teams